God's Word

as Therapy

Sharon Platt-McDonald
MSc, RHV, RM, RGN

Copyright © 2011
First Published 2011

ISBN number: 978-1-907244-11-7

British Library Cataloguing in Publication
Data. A catalogue record for this book is
available from the British Library.

All Bible quotations not attributed to
the New King James Version or the
New International Version come from the
King James Version, with a single
exception from the Message.

Published by Autumn House Publishing
(Europe) Ltd, Alma Park, Grantham,
Lincolnshire, England.

Design: Abigail Murphy

Printed in Thailand

The power of God's words

Life experiences have the capacity to affect our lives in proportion to our perception of events and the significance we attach to them. As Christians, we rely on God to keep us grounded among all the changes of life. Part of that stability is founded on the immutable Word of God, which provides healing for hurting hearts, peace for troubled minds, and restoration for both body and spirit.

To use God's Word is to use a powerful instrument. There is power not only in the written Word of God but also in the spoken Word. From the beginning of time – when God spoke 'and it was done' – to the transcription of the sixty-six books of the Bible which we now hold as a compass for life, we see the efficacy of the Word to effect change. We too, by God's grace, can speak into being the things we wish for our lives by applying the promises of God to our lives, for his Word is life-changing. Our application of God's Word in Jesus' name will always bring results.

In this book I examine the effect of words: the power of God's words to influence and transform our lives, and the healing we can receive when we apply his Word in our lives.

His Word

'In the beginning God . . .'
(Genesis 1:1)

I remember reading just those four words as a child and thinking how powerful they were. In that phrase there was, and is, a world of meaning which stimulated my love of words, and started my quest to analyse and explore the meanings buried within literary expression.

An analysis of Genesis soon brought the realisation that God started everything – therefore everything that comes after that is within the scope of his control. That was a mind-blowing discovery. It also gave me a love and awe of God's words, and the realisation that, since he was powerful enough to create the entirety of the heavens and the earth just by speaking them into being, then his words would have a significant impact even in my own life. I therefore can trust every word written in the Bible.

In the hallway of our home, on the wall by the front door, you can read the words of Scripture taken from Deuteronomy 28:6: '**Blessed shall you be when you come in, and blessed shall you be when you go out**' *(NKJV)*. Over the door, another sign reads: '**The LORD will keep you from all harm – he will watch over your life; the LORD will watch over your coming and going both now and forevermore.**' *(Psalm 121:7, 8, NIV.)*

Verses of Scripture can be found throughout our home. For example, in our kitchen one plaque bears the words: **'Blessed shall be your basket and your kneading bowl'** *(Deuteronomy 28:5, NKJV)*. In our prayer room, the door sign reads: **'Then you will call upon Me and go and pray to Me, and I will listen to you'** *(Jeremiah 29:12, NKJV)*.

We can find assurance from God's Word to suit every situation. The passage of Scripture in our hallway reminds us of God's protective care as we come and go each day. The kitchen passage of Scripture assures us that God will bless our provisions and daily food. And what confidence it gives me to know that, every time I pray, God will always hear me!

'He sent His word
and healed them,
And delivered them from
their destructions.'
(Psalm 107:20, NKJV)

From an early age I realised that
God's Word not only brought life:
it also continues to sustain life.
God's Word is indeed 'life' and
'health' *(Proverbs 4:22)*. The
Hebrew word 'health' can also be
translated 'medicine', 'cure',
'deliverance' or 'remedy'. God's
Word is therapy for the mind, body
and spirit, and has a positive,
medicinal effect on the sick. Better
still; God's therapy has no harmful
side-effects!

Just think of who God is and how he reflects his character through his Word and his Son, Jesus. You will have reason to praise him for the healing he brings.

He is the Chief Psychologist who says to us, **'Let this mind be in you, which was also in Christ Jesus'** *(Philippians 2:5)*.

God is an outstanding Optician

When you need to see your way, his Word will be a lamp unto your feet and a light unto your path.
(Psalm 119:105)

God is the best Ear Doctor

When you need a word in your ear, '. . . thine ears shall hear a word behind thee, saying, This is the way, walk ye in it' *(Isaiah 30:21)*.

God is a superb Speech Therapist

'. . . for I will give you a mouth and wisdom . . .' *(Luke 21:15, NKJV)*

His Word also teaches us to speak with grace *(Colossians 4:6)*.

God is the world-renowned Heart Surgeon

He performs the ultimate heart transplant – for he tells us, '**And I will give them one heart, and I will put a new spirit within you; and I will take the stony heart out of their flesh, and will give them an heart of flesh**' *(Ezekiel 11:19)*.

God is the greatest Orthopaedic Surgeon

He makes the lame to walk and leap for joy *(Isaiah 35:6)*.

He's an excellent Physiotherapist

He touched the paralytic and dormant limbs sprang into action *(Mark 2:1-12)*.

God is a skilled Paediatrician

He says, '**Let the little children come to Me**' *(Luke 18:16, NKJV)*.

He's the exceptional Gynaecologist

When no one else knew what to do, he healed the woman with the issue of blood *(Luke 8:43-48)*.

God is the best General Practitioner

If you've got a disease, he can heal it. Psalm 103:3 tells us he **'healeth all thy diseases'**.

God is a superb Diagnostician

'Before I formed you in the womb I knew you' *(Jeremiah 1:5, NKJV).*

He's the greatest Biologist

'. . . the LORD that made thee, and formed thee from the womb . . . will help thee' *(Isaiah 44:2).*

Words as therapeutic intervention

'Pleasant words are as an honeycomb, sweet to the soul, and health to the bones.' *(Proverbs 16:24)*

'For the word of God is living and powerful, and sharper than any two-edged sword, piercing even to the division of soul and spirit, and of joints and marrow, and is a discerner of the thoughts and intents of the heart.'
(Hebrews 4:12, NKJV)

Science also attests to the healing power of words – particularly words of Scripture. Recent studies have demonstrated that, in the context of Christian counselling, the application of Scripture in psychotherapy has been found to be effective, especially for trauma victims.

Some Christian therapists have been cautious of using Scripture with clients who expressed their faith during therapy; however, studies now demonstrate that treatments which incorporate the Bible can aid the healing process for Christian clients.

The research of several mental health institutions has associated improvements in mental health with certain aspects of religious and spiritual involvement. A study by the Mental Health Foundation found that religious people, particularly those who believe in a transcendent Being or higher power, are more likely to recover from depression. Prayer and the reading of Scripture were integral to their recovery.

The Royal College of Psychiatrists discovered that mental health service users found high-quality spiritual care to be beneficial. These service users reported improved self-control, higher self-esteem, increased confidence and better relationships.

'It is written, Man shall not live by
bread alone, but by every word that
proceedeth out of the mouth of God.'
(Matthew 4:4)

Bible survey

In June 2010 I undertook a survey of 150 Christians to ascertain the therapeutic benefits of the Word of God – the Bible.

The two survey questions I asked were:

- Is there any verse of Scripture that you find therapeutic?

- Why do you find it therapeutic; what has been its impact on you?

There were scores of responses, fifty of which I present in this book. I categorised the responses according to a number of themes.

The twenty-third Psalm was the text most frequently quoted. One respondent said, 'When I have had a stressful day and feel I haven't done half of what I set out to do, being led beside '**cool waters**' and having my '**soul restored**' is what I need – and the thought of having my head '**anointed with oil**' is just so soothing. Surely then I can recognise that, though the day has many frustrations, still I can truly say '**my cup runneth over**'!

Several other respondents found verse 4 of Psalm 23 a huge comfort, especially when faced with a serious or even terminal illness:

'Yea, though I walk through the valley
of the shadow of death,
I will fear no evil: for thou art with me;
thy rod and thy
staff they comfort me.'

A number of them are now enjoying perfectly good health, which attests to the healing power of the Psalm that they read every day and believe unequivocally.

Rest and restoration

A number of respondents chose Matthew 11:28-30. One individual stated; 'This is very therapeutic for me because I find it the ultimate panacea for stressed-out, anxious and depressed people endeavouring to keep pace with the ever-increasing demands of twenty-first century living . . . Jesus invites us to rest from all this – the anxiety of futile labour, heavy burdens, fear and depression.'

'Come unto me, all ye that labour and are heavy laden, and I will give you rest. Take my yoke upon you, and learn of me; for I am meek and lowly in heart: and ye shall find rest unto your souls. For my yoke is easy, and my burden is light.' *(Matthew 11:28-30)*

Another respondent chose the same passage of Scripture in a different translation. She explains: 'My therapeutic Scripture is Matthew 11:28-30 in the Message Bible:

"Are you tired? Worn out? Burned out on religion? Come to me. Get away with me and you'll recover your life. I'll show you how to take a real rest. Walk with me and work with me – watch how I do it. Learn the unforced rhythms of grace. I won't lay anything heavy or ill-fitting on you. Keep company with me and you'll learn to live freely and lightly."

'I feel peace just reading that verse, and I'm so grateful to God that he wants to help me to live freely and lightly. The text to me is a promise that, if I go to God, he is able to do so much for me. And I have found that it works – the best time-management course I know!'

Healing

This was a prominent theme among the respondents. One doctor gave several Scriptures that she found therapeutic. She writes: 'Where does one begin? The Bible is the most therapeutic of all books! As a teenager I found Matthew 11:28-30 (**"Come unto me all ye that labour . . ."**) very therapeutic for anxiety of all kinds. It prevented me from becoming a nervous wreck!

'And we know that all things work together for good to them that love God, to them who are the called according to his purpose.'
(Romans 8:28)

This verse provides healing for all sorts of worries – it can calm all fear.

'Make a joyful noise unto the LORD,
all ye lands.
Serve the LORD with gladness: come
before his presence with singing.
Know ye that the LORD he is God:
it is he that hath made us,
and not we ourselves;
we are his people,
and the sheep of his pasture.
Enter into his gates with thanksgiving,
and into his courts with praise:
be thankful unto him,
and bless his name.
For the LORD is good;
his mercy is everlasting;
and his truth endureth to
all generations.' *(Psalm 100)*

Insomnia sufferers have found this passage of Scripture to be particularly helpful:

> **'I will both lie down**
> **in peace, and sleep;**
> **For you alone, O LORD,**
> **make me dwell in safety.'**
> *(Psalm 4:8, NKJV)*

The fruit of the Spirit heals our
minds:

'. . . the fruit of the Spirit is love,
joy, peace, long-suffering,
kindness, goodness, faithfulness,
gentleness, self-control.
Against such there is no law.'
(Galatians 5:22, 23, NKJV)

Another respondent quotes a passage from Jeremiah, saying, 'Jeremiah 30:17 does it for me, because it's my promise of healing and restoration on many levels, and it can be applied to different life experiences':

'For I will restore health unto thee, and I will heal thee of thy wounds, saith the LORD'.

One participant said, 'When Jesus asked the lame man at the pool of Bethesda whether he wanted to be well, at first glance it may have seemed like a silly question: surely every sick person wants to be made whole! However, Christ's question may imply that the man was not making use of all the means available to get better, or perhaps he had given up hope of getting better. So whenever I fall ill or I am low in spirit, I always remember the words Jesus spoke, and I imagine Jesus is right in front of me asking a similar question.'

'When Jesus saw him lying there, and knew that he already had been in that condition a long time, He said to him, "Do you want to be made well?" '
(John 5:6, NKJV)

'Trust in the LORD with all thine heart; and lean not unto thine own understanding. In all thy ways acknowledge him, and he shall direct thy paths. Be not wise in thine own eyes: fear the LORD, and depart from evil. It shall be health to thy navel, and marrow to thy bones.' *(Proverbs 3:5-8)*

The respondent who quoted from Proverbs 3:5-8 explained; 'There are health benefits to trusting wholeheartedly in the LORD, reverencing him and determining to do no evil. If I ever feel arrogantly that I know it all, I am admonished not to trust in my own flawed wisdom and intelligence. If I rely on the LORD, I am promised **'health to my navel, and marrow to my bones'** – what a wonderful promise!

'Marrow is important, because it makes the red blood cells which carry oxygen to every part of your body, platelets which repair you, and white blood cells which fight infection. Without this we would all perish.'

Emotional support and healing for the mind

One respondent said, 'There are so many texts that provide emotional comfort. Here is one of my favourites that has kept me strong in faith as I have worked with people:'

'. . . God has said, "Never will I leave you; never will I forsake you." So we say with confidence, "The Lord is my helper; I will not be afraid. What can man do to me?" ' *(Hebrews 13:5, 6, NIV)*

'Often when I am afraid I repeat this text over and over again; sometimes I say it out loud and in front of a mirror. It is a call to tap into the empowerment and boldness that God gives us. It's there for the taking – we just have to claim it!'

'For God hath not given us the spirit of fear; but of power, and of love, and of a sound mind.' *(2 Timothy 1:7)*

Another respondent, again quoting 2 Timothy 1:7, said: 'When I am fearful, worried or perplexed, this text reminds me that God does not want me to feel this way. The ability to understand God's power and love with a sound mind just about covers everything I need to get through any issue.'

'So many Bible texts bring me comfort and healing – where do I begin? I used to struggle so much with negative thinking. But when I read Philippians 4:8 it focuses my mind on a positive place. It reminds me that there are no benefits to negativity. The more I stay positive and have a good attitude (despite my circumstances), the better I feel and the better I am!'

'Finally, brethren, whatsoever things are true, whatsoever things are honest, whatsoever things are just, whatsoever things are pure, whatsoever things are lovely, whatsoever things are of good report; if there be any virtue, and if there be any praise, think on these things.' *(Philippians 4:8)*

Continuing to mention texts that promote positive thinking, the same respondent quoted 1 Thessalonians 5:18, saying: 'When I remember to give thanks and to make a habit of doing this, I'm less inclined to be negative about myself, others or circumstances, and even (dare I say it) less inclined to be negative about God's leading. This is a joy text!'

'In every thing give thanks: for this is the will of God in Christ Jesus concerning you.' *(1 Thessalonians 5:18)*

Here is another joy text, as the respondent goes on to explain on the next page:

'Casting down imaginations, and every high thing that exalteth itself against the knowledge of God, and bringing into captivity every thought to the obedience of Christ'
(2 Corinthians 10:5).

'. . . this text [on the previous page] encourages me that I don't have to be a victim of my own thoughts. I have control. I can do something about my thought processes. I can bring my thoughts in line with God's, choosing to relinquish my own, which in this context are usually negative. This is a conscious decision to stop rehearsing old ways of faulty thinking, imaginations, reasons, faults, blame, guilt and so on. This is really powerful, and it works for me!'

'When I feel like I can't go on anymore, that I don't have what it takes, this text reminds me that doing things God's way will strengthen me. With him I can go the extra mile, rising above challenges to overcome them. Sometimes you just have to do what you can, recognising that you may have to walk, not run; but just keep on going and the strength to soar will come.'

'But they that wait upon the LORD shall renew their strength; they shall mount up with wings as eagles; they shall run, and not be weary; and they shall walk, and not faint.' *(Isaiah 40:31)*

Peace and emotional well-being

This was another key area in the survey. One respondent states: 'I prayed for and experienced that peace of God which I can't explain when my sister was diagnosed with cancer. The medical staff could not understand how calm and serene we were. This text has since brought great comfort to me in times of stress.'

'Be anxious for nothing, but in everything by prayer and supplication, with thanksgiving, let your requests be made known to God; and the peace of God, which surpasses all understanding, will guard your hearts and minds through Christ Jesus.'
(Philippians 4:6-7, NKJV)

Confronting fear

'This was a text the Lord gave me when I was taking my GCE exams. I remember walking to my first exam feeling so nervous. My legs were going forward to school but my mind was in terror and was returning home. It was a most strange feeling. That evening, when revising, I shared my fear with the Lord. I then remembered that my Grandma once shared with me the fact that in times of need she would ask the Lord to give her a text in answer to her prayer.'

**'Surely God is my salvation;
I will trust and not be afraid. The LORD,
the LORD, is my strength and my song;
he has become my salvation.'**
(Isaiah 12:2, NIV)

'. . . Getting my Bible, I held it in a closed position and, as I prayed, I let it open. I then put my finger on the page and read the text it was on. It was Isaiah 12:2. Knowing that God answered my plea for help, I did not fear the exam or the results. I even passed Biology, a subject with which I struggled. Later on, I needed a science subject to be able to do the degree which launched me into becoming, firstly, an associate in pastoral care and then, for the last 17 years, a church department director for children's, family and women's ministries.'

'Often, when single, as a wife and as a mother, this text has come to mind when fear makes me anxious. The result of this promise is shown in the following verses, which say that trusting in God will bring joy and the happiness of praising the LORD to everyone you meet. I rejoice today that God does keep his promises, and that makes my day-to-day life so much less stressful.'

'With joy you will draw water from the wells of salvation. In that day you will say: "Give thanks to the LORD, call on his name; make known among the nations what he has done, and proclaim that his name is exalted." '
(Isaiah 12:3, 4, NIV)

Guidance and life direction

A number of texts from the Old Testament surfaced in this field. Several respondents to the survey quoted Jeremiah 29:11 and Proverbs 3:5, 6 as the therapeutic Scriptures which guided them in times of anxiety.

One respondent says, 'If I am tempted to worry about the future, this verse reassures me that God wants only what is good for me:'

' "For I know the plans I have for you," declares the LORD, "plans to prosper you and not to harm you, plans to give you hope and a future." '
(Jeremiah 29:11, NIV)

Another respondent states, 'One of my favourite texts is Proverbs 3:5, 6. This text has helped me to be emotionally strong: especially when I was doing my nurse training for the first part of the three years. I faced some serious hardship, the toughest time I ever went through. This experience has taught me how to trust God's heart when I can't see his hand.'

'Trust in the LORD with all your heart,
And lean not on your own understanding;
In all your ways acknowledge Him,
And He shall direct your paths.'
(Proverbs 3:5, 6, NKJV)

Commenting on Proverbs 3:5, 6, another individual writes, 'When there seem to be no solutions to life's problems, this verse gives me the assurance I need – that God is in control and I do not need to worry:'

'The LORD Almighty has sworn, "Surely, as I have planned, so it will be, and as I have purposed, so it will stand . . . ." For the LORD Almighty has purposed, and who can thwart him? His hand is stretched out, and who can turn it back?' *(Isaiah 14:24, 27, NIV)*

Life expectations

'Philippians 4:13 tells me exactly what it says: I can do all things through Christ, as I am not relying on my own strength, but on that of the LORD God Almighty. I find this therapeutic, as I need not struggle through life attempting to progress in my own strength. I ask my Father for help, as he is always with me.'

'I can do all things through Christ who strengthens me.' *(Philippians 4:13, NKJV)*

God's provision and answers for our lives

'It is comforting to know that God is always available, listening and speaking to me as I call upon him. That's better than calling any friend and getting their voicemail, texting only to receive a reply a day or two later, or ringing when your friends are out.'

'And it shall come to pass, that before they call, I will answer; and while they are yet speaking, I will hear.'
(Isaiah 65:24)

'This psalm makes me understand that even though the present may be challenging, God is not taking from me anything that is good. If he takes something, it's probably not good for me to have it. We live in such an uncertain time, but God is my Shield and he helps me to be positive and happy. He is in control and I have no reason to stress, but to trust in his wisdom.'

'For the LORD God is a sun and shield: the LORD will give grace and glory: no good thing will he withhold from them that walk uprightly.' *(Psalm 84:11)*

God's word as protection and guidance

'This Scripture offers me the greatest assurance of God's guidance, now and forevermore:'

'Thou art my hiding place; thou shalt preserve me from trouble; thou shalt compass me about with songs of deliverance. . . . I will instruct thee and teach thee in the way which thou shalt go: I will guide thee with mine eye.'
(Psalm 32:7, 8)

God's thoughts

'It does me good to know what God thinks, and that he will always be with me: this is totally priceless.'

'How precious also are Your thoughts to me, O God! How great is the sum of them! If I should count them, they would be more in number than the sand; When I awake, I am still with You.' *(Psalm 139:17, 18, NKJV)*

Another respondent writes, 'The entire Word of God is soothing to me. However, the verses that break my heart and renew my joy in Jesus are found in Romans:'

'And hope maketh not ashamed; because the love of God is shed abroad in our hearts by the Holy Ghost which is given unto us. For when we were yet without strength, in due time Christ died for the ungodly. For scarcely for a righteous man will one die: yet peradventure for a good man some would even dare to die. But God commendeth his love toward us, in that, while we were yet sinners, Christ died for us.' *(Romans 5:5-8)*

'The truth expressed in Romans 5:5-8 brings such healing to my soul as I think of the pure, deep love of God. The Holy Ghost has truly revealed the love of God and shed it abroad in my heart in such a way that it has healed me from fears, disappointments, sadness, frustration, criticism, negative thoughts and feelings towards others, spiritual blindness, impatience, lethargy, foolish talk, and everything else that would otherwise imprison me in this dark world of sin.'

Romans 5:5-8 tells me that as long as **I am in Christ** and **Christ is in me**, I am made whole, and it is this hope that will never make us ashamed or put us to shame. The experience of the Gospel is healing in every way. Praise God!'

How God works for us

Imagine leaving the hard work of analysing life, with all its changes and challenges, to God: he is never taken by surprise, but knows the outcome ahead of time.

'And we know that all things work together for good to them that love God, to them who are the called according to his purpose.'
(Romans 8:28)

Commenting on Romans 8:28, our respondent said: 'Everyone has an ideal for their life – how many kids they want, when they want to get married, their work or profession, their involvement in the Church, their house or car and so on – but things do not always go the way they planned. Sometimes I feel like nothing is working out for me in the way I want it to; everything seems to be going wrong in my life and I go through so much pain and suffering alongside of it. Often I ask God, "How much longer do I have to wait until your coming? Come now!" '

'Romans 8:28 helps me to wait patiently for Christ's return, and continues to give me that hope and assurance that everything will be just fine. I am reminded that Christ suffered when he was here. We too, his children, will also go through suffering until he comes. It calms my spirit and gets rid of all the doubts, fears and anguish I may experience.'

Another survey participant relayed her choice: 'My text is found in Exodus 14. Whenever I feel that the whole world is crumbling around me, I remember when the Israelites were at the Red Sea with nowhere to go. They had no hope and, about to give up, they started accusing Moses. This spectacular response, which Moses gave, always gives me hope:'

'And Moses said to the people, "Do not be afraid. Stand still, and see the salvation of the LORD, which He will accomplish for you today. For the Egyptians whom you see today, you shall see again no more forever. The LORD will fight for you, and you shall hold your peace." '
(Exodus 14:13, 14, NKJV)

Eternal hope

Just imagine a world without suffering! It's out of this world – literally. One survey participant shares her therapeutic Scripture:

'And God shall wipe away all tears from their eyes; and there shall be no more death, neither sorrow, nor crying, neither shall there be any more pain: for the former things are passed away.'
(Revelation 21:4)

She goes on to explain: 'There has been a spate of funerals recently, and the older I get, the more funerals I attend. Life sometimes can be painful, full of tears, sorrow, disappointment and loss. The older we get, the more our earthen vessels fail. That was the price which we, through the first Adam, paid for taking a bite out of that forbidden fruit. That emptiness you feel, that loneliness, that internal and unending need to plug a gap: that gap was once filled intimately by God's presence and can only be filled by him again.'

God promises a new thing. That new thing will ultimately be a new Heaven and a new Earth; the former things will pass away, and there will be an end to tears, death, sorrow, crying and pain – the start of a new beginning at which we will once again be united with our heavenly Father. Now that's healing!

'Forget the former things; do not dwell on the past. See, I am doing a new thing! Now it springs up; do you not perceive it? I am making a way in the desert and streams in the wasteland.'
(Isaiah 43:18, 19, NIV)

Trust in God

'Do not be anxious about anything, but in everything, by prayer and petition, with thanksgiving, present your requests to God. And the peace of God, which transcends all understanding, will guard your hearts and your minds in Christ Jesus.' *(Philippians 4:6, 7, NIV)*

While on a holiday with my father in Jamaica, we experienced a hurricane. We had gone to the beach the previous day. Several people noted that the clouds appeared to be moving quickly across the sky. By the next day, severe weather warnings were being aired.

My uncle, with whom I was staying, had been running around all day securing his neighbours' homes while leaving his own home unattended. The evening news reported that the hurricane was approaching the island at ninety-five miles per hour. The wind was already very strong. There was still no sign of my uncle. To make matters worse, my father had gone to visit relatives, so I was left alone in the house.

Needless to say, my uncle arrived 'at the eleventh hour'. With the help of neighbours, the roof, windows and door were secured. The storm began.

The events which followed were like a nightmare. During the hurricane, a large pear tree fell across the house. The electricity was cut off. The entire island was in darkness for several hours.

Throughout the three-day storm, I had no idea what had happened to my father.

The text we used for our worship was:

'Be careful for nothing; but in everything by prayer and supplication with thanksgiving let your requests be made known unto God. And the peace of God, which passeth all understanding, shall keep your hearts and minds through Christ Jesus.'
(Philippians 4:6, 7)

I held onto those words for dear life, and gave God thanks that he was in God's hands.

The storm passed. The damage was significant, but our lives were spared. My father had sought shelter with relatives for the duration of the storm, and, when it **was** all over, we were re-united. God had answered our prayers. We saw also that, when we trust God's Word, it brings us peace.

That experience reminds me of the unpredictability of life, and of the anxiety we face when storms arise in our lives. God reminds us through his Word that he is still in charge, and, if we call out to him, he will hear and answer us.

Hearing from God

'And it shall come to pass, that before they call, I will answer; and while they are yet speaking, I will hear.' *(Isaiah 65:24)*

I was once one of those cynical young ladies who felt that, as far as 'good' men were concerned, the land was barren. Having come out of a broken engagement I was very cautious. I prayed that one day the Lord would provide a God-fearing husband.

One Sabbath, Denzle invited me for a walk after church. We enjoyed our time talking together. He asked me to go on a date.

Seven years previously, he had 'asked me out', but I had declined. This time around, it felt quite different.

I needed time to put the request before God. I wanted God to tell me whether this was the one. I asked Denzle whether he would join me in fasting and praying about our decision – and so we did. A date was set for the following week. I asked if we could pray every hour, on the hour, and then meet up at the prayer meeting, where – I felt sure! – we would come to a decision.

On that morning, I had an exciting sense that God was going to speak to me. There was no agreement about how we should pray or what we should read.

At 10am I entered the bathroom to pray. I poured out my heart to God more passionately than at 7, 8 or 9am.

I also asked that Denzle might feel God's anointing. To my surprise, my eyes rested on 1 Samuel 16:11-13. I reached verse 12:

'. . .And the LORD said, "Arise, anoint him; for this is the one!" Then Samuel took the horn of oil and anointed him in the midst of his brothers; and the Spirit of the LORD came upon David from that day forward. . .' *(1 Samuel 16:12-13, NKJV)*

I felt that somehow God was speaking to me: I prayed that God would speak to both Denzle and myself, and that when we met that evening there would be no doubt as to what God was saying to both of us.

That evening, I went to the prayer meeting with a little more eagerness than usual. At the end of the prayer meeting I got up and made my way down the aisle. I could see Denzle waving frantically from the back of the church. He was beaming as he approached me.

'Sharon, ten o'clock today! Oh man, what an experience!' I immediately sat down on the bench as my knees had gone weak. I knew what I had experienced at 10am that morning, and was surprised to hear that he appeared to have had a significant experience at the same time. I asked him what had happened at 10am.

He stated that the early morning prayer session had gone well. However, at 10am he felt particularly impressed to pour out his heart to God.

He was driving at the time, and was compelled to park the car and pray. His prayer was that God would reveal himself by making his Presence felt right there and then, and that, like David, he might experience the anointing of God! As he did so, he recalled that he felt an overwhelming Presence, a sensation of heat from the top of his head right down to his feet. As he prayed further, he asked God to speak through his Word, and, as he opened the Bible, his eyes fell on 1 Samuel 16:11-13.

Denzle was just as flabbergasted as I was when he heard of what I too had experienced at the same time. We gave thanks.

Heavenly assistance

**'Are they not all ministering spirits,
sent forth to minister for them
who shall be heirs of salvation?'**
(Hebrews 1:14)

It was 'baby clinic' day, which
meant that I had to see a long line
of mothers with their infants. As
usual, the clinic was running late,
with too many clients and not
enough health professionals. At
the end of the clinic – just as I was
clearing up – a woman walked in.
From the look on her face, I could
tell that this was going to take a
long time! Two hours later, after
listening to her plight, I asked her
if we could pray together. I then
made arrangements to see her the
next week.

Tired and hungry, I left the clinic thankful that I could be there for someone in need. It was my intention to visit the Christian bookshop and buy a small booklet which would adequately address some of the issues the woman shared with me.

When I arrived at the bookshop, I went to pick out the booklet. I stopped to greet two children. They looked quite dishevelled.

The young girl pulled out a book from the children's section and handed it to me. The boy asked me to read a story for them. Glancing at the time, I told them I would have to be quick. We sat down. I read a short chapter, and then got up to announce my departure.

They left. I headed to the counter to pay for my booklet. However, when I searched my handbag, my purse was nowhere to be found! I felt a sense of panic. What was I going to do? Sensing my bewilderment, the shopkeeper asked me if something was wrong. I explained to him that my purse had gone missing. He asked me whether I had spoken to anyone since I came in. It was then that I remembered the children.

The shopkeeper confirmed my fears. There had been a spate of thefts in the shop recently – including pick-pocketing. The children had been banned from the shop, but that day they must have slipped in unnoticed.

Silently I challenged God: 'Lord, how could you let this happen to me? Here I am foregoing my lunch break to help someone in need, and I come into a Christian bookshop only to suffer the theft of the little money I had left for the month – and that while I was helping those whom I thought to be innocent children!' I cried.

A few customers came to encourage me. I noticed a man standing a distance away, but he did not appear to notice me. Even when I came closer, to give the shop manager my details, the gentleman appeared not to notice me. He turned to leave. I too made my way towards the door.

The gentleman turned around and said, 'God is watching.' Then, noticing my inquiring look, he stated: 'God has seen, God has heard.' I was rather surprised at this. He then took out his wallet and held out a five-pound note. I stepped back in surprise! 'God has asked me to give you this', he said.

I hesitated. Again, he extended the money towards me. Not used to taking anything from strangers, I felt uncomfortable. I rummaged through my bag for a pen to take down his contact details, asking, 'How can I return it to you? Which church do you attend?' He replied, 'God wants you to have it.'

I looked more closely at him, and found myself asking his name. He did not respond at first, but looked at me as if to ask why I needed to know that. After a pause, he said, 'Jim'. Immediately, I remembered the recent Christian posters that had asked, 'Have you seen JIM lately?' ('JIM' stood for Jesus In Me.) I held his gaze as I realised that 'Jim' was not his real name. He looked away.

'I'll see you in Heaven', he said.

It dawned on me that this was no ordinary person.

I looked down momentarily before heading after him. He had literally just stepped outside; the door was closing behind him, and I was only a few steps away. But when I opened the door, I looked left, right, and across the road – he was nowhere to be seen. I looked in the adjacent shops on either side: no sign of him. I stepped out into the street to look further down the road. There had been no parked cars around, so he couldn't have left by car; no buses had passed during that short time, and neither was he standing outside a bus stop.

It was then that I realised: maybe, just maybe, this could have been a heavenly visitation.

Faith in the dark

'And my God shall supply all your need according to His riches in glory by Christ Jesus' *(Philippians 4:19, NKJV)*

We had moved house. The property wasn't quite what we had dreamed. However, it was affordable, and had lots of potential. We busied ourselves with the modernisation. The required work was more intensive than we had understood from the survey, and took more time and money than we had hoped.

A short time later, along with six of his colleagues, my husband was made redundant.

Even in our disappointment, we realised that we had to trust God to provide for us. We were living on one wage with a lot of work still needed on the house.

We had decided some time previously to have a 'praise party' to take us into the New Year. The news of the redundancy had not put us in a celebratory mood; however, we felt that we still had much for which to thank God. Coming together in prayer, my husband and I told God that we would celebrate him just as if all our finances and jobs were secure. Each day in our worship, we would read the Scripture from Philippians 4:19, including it in our prayers.

The party went ahead. It was a testimony of trusting God in the dark. Later, we looked back and recalled the many promise texts and Scripture games we played at the party.

There were many difficult moments when we could not see our way or make any long-term plans, due to our uncertainty about our finances. It was a dark time. Bills were paid, albeit sometimes a little late.

The Lord provided a job for my husband, and our fears were allayed. We learned that to practise faith is to trust when you cannot see; for God does the 'seeing' for us.

At the time of writing, we are facing a similar situation. The worldwide economic downturn has made its effects known, and we have felt the repercussions of the uncertainties of life. Twenty-three months ago, my husband's boss announced the closure of his company.

So here we are, with only one regular salary for the last twenty-three months; once again trusting in God to supply our urgent needs. This time around, we are a little more trusting.

'We have nothing to fear for the future, except as we shall forget the way the Lord has led us.' *(Ellen White)*

Trying times

'When you pass through the waters,
I will be with you;
And through the rivers,
they shall not overflow you.
When you walk through the fire,
you shall not be burned,
Nor shall the flame scorch you.
For I am the LORD your God . . .'
(Isaiah 43:2, 3, NKJV)

2002 was one of those years that
will forever be etched on my
memory. It was a year of intense
challenge for our family.

In the May of 2002, my mother collapsed at camp meeting. We had grave concerns about her health, as she had suffered two brain haemorrhages in the past, during which God had miraculously spared her life.

Shortly afterwards, we received news of other family illnesses. My mother's youngest brother became seriously ill and spent several months in hospital before passing away.

Another uncle had open-heart surgery, and subsequently developed complications.

During this traumatic period, we discovered that my youngest sister had a potentially cancerous lump in her neck.

Following my sister's surgery, my husband and I decided that her recovery would be eased if she came to live with us for a while. I was able to nurse my sister during her recovery. This meant that my other sister could look after my mother.

We were quite concerned about how my mother would take the news of my sister's diagnosis: she was quite frail.

It was a time of immense stress. I remember, during a moment of frustration, questioning God's wisdom and timing. It all came to a head one Sabbath morning.

The phone rang and we received the shocking news of my uncle's death. My sister was due to be discharged that afternoon. He was my sister's favourite uncle. I felt that it would break her heart at a time when she had only just come to terms with her own diagnosis. Surely things couldn't get any worse.

Within minutes of receiving the news of my uncle's death, my husband received a call which told him that his aunt had been diagnosed with cancer and given a very poor prognosis. It felt as though sickness and death were all around us.

It was at this time that I cried out to God, asking him how much more he thought we could take. Then I remembered Job. I recalled the series of devastating events that he endured in quick succession, culminating in his own physical affliction: yet he could declare, in Job 13:15, **'Though he slay me, yet will I trust in him'**. I told myself that, with God's help, if Job could survive his trauma, so could we.

With grieving hearts, we went to church. We gained great comfort from the church members when the news of my uncle's death and my sister's cancer was shared with them. I remember looking across to my mother in church, and wondering how she would come through this.

Reflectively, I turned to Isaiah 43:2, 3, and read (in the NKJV):

'When you pass through the waters,
I will be with you;
And through the rivers,
they shall not overflow you.
When you walk through the fire,
you shall not be burned,
Nor shall the flame scorch you.
For I am the LORD your God . . .'

As I read these words, I wept, realising God's promise.

We did not drown in the stormy waters of 2002; we came through them. Today – thank God! – my sister is enjoying good health, and my mother is sustained.

You too may be facing challenges that seem overwhelming: but don't panic! Wait for God's breakthrough; for we truly serve an awesome God.

Travel trauma

'The eternal God is your refuge, and underneath are the everlasting arms . . .' *(Deuteronomy 33:27, NIV)*

March 10 2008 is a date that will be forever etched on the minds of my husband Denzle and I.

We were returning home to the UK from a training event in the US. A severe weather warning had been in effect for a few days, and some flights into the UK had already been cancelled prior to our departure. However, on the evening when we arrived at the airport, our flight took off as scheduled.

The flight was unusually turbulent, and we were told to keep our seatbelts on. I don't like flying at the best of times, and so I was a little tense (but not panicked) while I travelled with my husband. He loves flying. More importantly though, upon each flight we would always commit the journey to God for his divine protection.

We were on the plane, due to land in two hours' time. We realised we were heading directly into a storm. What had been a turbulent flight soon became very turbulent, and we were requested to stay in our seats for the rest of the flight with our seatbelts securely fastened.

As we made our descent, it was clear that we had hit the most violent part of the storm. The plane was being tossed back and forth. It was then that the pilot made his first announcement. He stated: 'It is beyond our capacity to land this plane safely; we may have to divert.'

As several other flights were also being diverted due to the storm, we were kept in a holding pattern until the flight path became clear, allowing us to proceed to Amsterdam: but things did not go according to plan. In fact, the situation was about to become very much worse, as we found out when the pilot made his second announcement . . .

After hovering for some time, awaiting the 'all clear' for landing, the pilot announced, 'We are almost out of fuel, so we will have to descend to see if we can make an attempted landing.' This time, an audible gasp was heard around the cabin. An attempted landing – in the very same weather in which the pilot had previously stated it was 'beyond his capacity to land the plane safely'?

For over fifteen minutes, we were thrown around in the air; overhead lockers shed their contents, oxygen masks descended, and the plane vibrated and shook violently, thrusting back and forth with huge jolts, repeatedly plunging several hundred feet at a time. It was truly terrifying.

My bag flew out from under my seat as I was almost ejected from where I was sitting. I shrieked in fright as Denzle grabbed me and held me close to him. I was convinced that, due to the force of the extreme ninety-mile-per-hour winds, the plane was going down. As I looked around, I could see pale faces, red eyes and visible signs of distress. Attempting to re-assure me, Denzle embraced me, saying, 'If we go down, I'll go down protecting you'!

Well that did it – the happy-go-lucky, confident Denzle, normally the eternal optimist, thought the plane was going to crash!

We began to pray earnestly that God might spare our lives. I was praying and crying, telling God that I was not ready to die yet. Then I remembered all the health resources that we were bringing back from the US for our health promotion programmes in our church and community, and I began to plead with God for an extension of life so that we could complete his work. Strange things come to mind at life-threatening moments.

I began to brace myself for the impending impact. Denzle, again attempting to reassure me, said, 'At least when they find us we will be together'! I changed my prayer and began asking God to accept me and to receive us into his Kingdom. I began taking deep breaths as I tried to relax and prepare for the inevitable.

I began to quote every text of Scripture I knew about God's protection: Psalm 121 seemed to be the one that I repeated most; in particular verse 7 (NKJV):

> **'The LORD shall preserve
> you from all evil;
> He shall preserve your soul.'**

It was at that point of relaxing, that final point of giving up my right to live, that I accepted God's will, whatever it would be. The struggle had been intense, and I felt a sense of relief as I set aside my own will in favour of God's. As I closed my eyes, I saw an image of a large hand on the underside of the plane – almost cushioning it. I heard the words 'This is enough', and the hand gently began to move upwards, almost as if it were lifting the plane above the maelstrom. At that very moment, we felt the plane lift as if it were being slowly pushed steadily upwards in a controlled motion. It was surreal!

After the plane lifted, we heard a breathless pilot make his third announcement, in broken sentences, as if coming back from an ordeal: 'Well . . . that was close . . . we are going to try heading back to Amsterdam now, as it's too dangerous to land. We just hope the fuel will hold up.'

Great! Just as I was beginning to pull myself together, there we were, faced with the possibility that we might plummet to the ground if the fuel ran out. Yet I could not forget the image of the plane being held in the huge hand, and I felt that God had literally cushioned the plane from the elements, saving us from certain death.

Eventually, 800 feet from the ground, with the pilot struggling to keep the aircraft under control, we were able to make another ascent and divert to Amsterdam, where the winds were a little calmer. However, as we had not received prior clearance to land in Amsterdam, there was a lengthy delay while we circled the airport awaiting landing instructions.

As we waited to land, the pilot announced that, due to the exceptional circumstances in which we found ourselves, we could use our mobile phones to contact our loved ones. I shivered as I realised the significance of that statement. Usually, while flying, the use of mobile phones is not permitted. But there we were, being allowed to make telephone calls while still airborne! I remember saying to Denzle, 'I wonder if he is allowing us this call because he thinks there's a possibility we won't make it back?'

As we landed in Amsterdam, an air hostess rushed towards the front of the plane carrying an oxygen cylinder to assist a passenger who was suffering a panic attack.

The cabin crew admitted, while we were being refuelled, that it had been a close call. One air hostess stated that it had been the worst air turbulence and attempted landing she had ever experienced. When asked if she was frightened, she said simply, 'Yes, I was.'

The pilot kept us updated while we stood in line to be refuelled after the other planes which had diverted ahead of us. He expressed concern that the winds were still at high speed, and told us that we would not attempt re-entry until the storm had abated and it was safer to fly.

Passengers on mobile phones were reporting the state of the weather and its repercussions back home: the roof damage, the school closures and all the flights cancelled at the airports. Some were asking why the flight had been allowed to take off when the weather reports had been so severe.

After we refuelled in Amsterdam, another attempt was made to land at Gatwick, and thankfully we landed safely. It was a very unsteady landing, as the plane swerved from side to side on the runway due to the force of the winds. As we skidded from side to side, my usual fear came back. I thought to myself, 'We escaped danger in the air only to face it on the ground!' You could hear the plane going into reverse throttle as the aircraft struggled to slow to a stop. The winds were so strong that, even after we came to a stop, the plane was still being rocked on the runway.

As we disembarked, walking past a quiet, solemn crew, a passenger asked one of the pilots: 'Can I ask you, was it touch and go back there when we attempted to land the first time?' The pilot paused, and then nodded: 'Yes – yes, it was.'

I felt once again the power of a mighty God, who literally holds the whole world in his hands; the words of that special passage of Scripture came back to me:

**'The eternal God is your refuge,
And underneath are the
everlasting arms . . .'**
(Deuteronomy 33:27, NKJV)

Conclusion

'And they overcame him by the blood of the Lamb and by the word of their testimony, and they did not love their lives to the death.'
(Revelation 12:11, NJKV)

As you read these testimonies of the power of God's Word in various 'seasons' of your life, do they touch a chord with you? Are there texts of Scripture which affect your life, which become vividly relevant to you in a particular season? If so – cherish them, hold them dear to your heart, for indeed God's Word is a lamp unto our feet and a light unto our path (Psalm 119:105).

His Word illuminates our journey and brightens the way before us.

I'm grateful to God for the experiences he has given me so far in my Christian journey. There have been times of great sorrow and challenges, as well as great joy and success. Yet I can attest to God's leadership at every stage. I thank him for guiding the journey thus far, and trust his leadership for the future.

I know I would not have made it through had it not been for the powerful, sustaining and healing words of God that not only carried me through challenging times but enabled me to look back with wonder at his leading. His words anchor my faith in him and give me hope for the future.

I have also learnt that, whatever the season of life, attitude makes all the difference. God's Word helps us to formulate an attitude of trust and confidence in his leading. If we 'rest' in God, we can see the lesson that he is trying to teach us with each life event. We need to remember that God uses even those occurrences which we may deem setbacks in order to move us forward.

Christ is preparing a place for us, and also preparing us for that place. May all our life experiences shape us for eternity as he perfects each season of our lives.

'So Jesus said to them, ". . . if you
have faith as a mustard seed, you
will say to this mountain, 'move from
here to there,' and it will move; and
nothing will be impossible for you." '
(Matthew 17:20, NKJV)

'. . . Thus says the LORD to you:
"Do not be afraid nor dismayed
because of this great multitude, for
the battle is not yours, but God's"'
(2 Chronicles 20:15, NKJV)

'. . . Do not let your heart faint, do not be afraid, and do not tremble or be terrified because of them; for the LORD your God is He who goes with you . . .'
(Deuteronomy 20:3, 4, NKJV)

'Peace I leave with you, My peace I give to you; not as the world gives do I give to you. Let not your heart be troubled, neither let it be afraid.'
(John 14:27, NKJV)

' "You will not need to fight in this battle. Position yourselves, stand still and see the salvation of the LORD, who is with you . . ." Do not fear or be dismayed . . .' *(2 Chronicles 20:17, NKJV)*

Prayers

O God, thank you for instilling faith in us, that even in the face of contrary opinions, we can trust in the power of your Word; we can believe the impossible, for with you all things are possible.

Dear God, I am grateful to you that you are faithful to us even when our faith fails. Thank you for the assurance that you will always meet our needs. Help us to hold on to the promises of your Word, for they never fail.

'For God has not given us a spirit of fear, but of power and of love and of a sound mind' *(2 Timothy 1:7, NKJV)*

'I will not leave you comfortless:
I will come to you.' *(John 14:18)*

'I write unto you, little children, because your sins are forgiven you for his name's sake.' *(1 John 2:12)*

'Let the words of my mouth and the
meditation of my heart
Be acceptable in Your sight,
O LORD, my strength and my
Redeemer.' *(Psalm 19:14, NKJV)*